Sarah's Choice

PHOENIX POETS
A Series Edited by Robert von Hallberg

Sarah's Choice

Eleanor Wilner

The University of Chicago Press
Chicago and London

ELEANOR WILNER is the author of two books of poems, *maya,* winner of
the 1979 Juniper Prize, and *Shekhinah,* published by the University of Chicago
Press.

THE UNIVERSITY OF CHICAGO PRESS, CHICAGO 60637
THE UNIVERSITY OF CHICAGO PRESS, LTD., LONDON
© 1989 by The University of Chicago
All rights reserved. Published 1989
Printed in the United States of America

98 97 96 95 94 93 92 91 90 89   54321

Library of Congress Cataloging in Publication Data

Wilner, Eleanor.
    Sarah's choice / Eleanor Wilner.
        p.   cm.—(Phoenix poets)
    I. Title.   II. Series.
    PS3573.I45673S2   1989
    811'.54—dc19   88-23317
    ISBN 0-226-90027-4.   ISBN 0-226-90028-2 (pbk.)   CIP

        ⊗   The paper used in this publication meets
        the minimum requirements of the American National
        Standard for Information Sciences—Permanence of
        Paper for Printed Library Materials, ANSI Z39.48-1984.

Listen, Cordelia. If a God had made the world, might would always be right, that would be so wise, we'd be spared so much suffering. But we made the world—out of our smallness and weakness. Our lives are awkward and fragile and we have only one thing to keep us sane: pity, and the man without pity is mad.

—from Edward Bond's LEAR

Acknowledgments

Some of the poems in this collection first appeared in the following periodicals or anthologies, and are reprinted with permission:

American Poetry Review 15, no. 1 (Jan. 23, 1986). "Homage to the River," "Minor Epic"

Aperture 94 (Spring 1984): 32. "Tucson Gardens"

Axe Factory Review 1, no. 1: 47. "Looking Back at Yeats"

Boulevard 2, no. 3 (Sept. 15, 1987): 110–12. "Going the Rounds"

Calyx: A Journal of Art & Literature by Women 10, no. 2/3 (Spring 1987); 8, no. 3 (Fall/Winter 1984). "Infection in the Ear," "The Last Man," "Two Pairs of Eyes"

Feminist Studies 10, no. 1 (1984): 59–64. "Postscript"

Four Contemporary Poets (New York: La Vida Press, 1984). "A Tale That's Best for Winter"

New Yorker (Nov. 14, 1988). "As Far As It Goes, and Back"

Northwest Review 22, no. 1/2 (1984). "High Noon at Los Alamos"

Poetry Kanto (Japan) 4 (Aug. 1987). "Beauty and the Beast"

Poetry Now (England) 6 (Summer 1986): 36–37. "Miriam's Song" (in an earlier version, " 'It's a Boy!' ")

Third Wind (Spring 1984): 80–90. "Reading the Bible Backwards," "Time Out of Mind"

TriQuarterly (Winter 1989). "Conversation with a Japanese Student," "It's Not Cold Here"

Many thanks to the Pennsylvania Council on the Arts, whose literary fellowship helped me in the completion of this manuscript. And to those good friends whose careful reading of the draft improved the work.

Contents

I UNBOUND
Coda, Overture   3
Reading the Bible Backwards   5
Miriam's Song   8
The Anabasis of Koré   10
Minor Epic   13
Desert Parable   15
Time Out of Mind   18
Sarah's Choice   21

II COMPANIONS
Postscript   27
Going the Rounds   30
Homage to the River   33
Tucson Gardens   35
The American Sublime: Robert Penn Warren   37
The Autumn of the Poets   39
"He was the whitest white man . . ."   41
"Never Apologize for Poetry"   44
"Into the Distance Where All Things Reverse and Touch"   46
Two Pairs of Eyes   48

III LAMENTATIONS
There Are Such Mornings   53
Beauty and the Beast   55
The Last Man   57
Colloquy with Medea   59
Infection in the Ear   61
As Far As It Goes, and Back   62
Gaijin Lament   64
High Noon at Los Alamos   66
Nandin's Tail   68
The Towers of Silence   70

IV RETURNS

Classical Proportions of the Heart   77

A Tale That's Best for Winter   80

Sunset on the Pembrokeshire Cliff Path   84

On the Place of Theory in an Obsolete Poetics   85

Looking Back at Yeats   87

It's Not Cold Here   89

"Midway the journey of this life . . ."   91

Still Waters   93

The Green Connection   95

Conversation with a Japanese Student   97

Having Eaten of the Tree of Knowledge   100

NOTES   101

I Unbound

Coda, Overture

She stepped out of the framing circle of the dark.
We thought, as she approached, to see her
clearly, but her features only grew more indistinct
as she drew nearer, like those of statues
long submerged in water. We couldn't name her,
she who can't be seen

except in spaces between wars, brief intervals

when history relents, reflection
intervenes, returning home
becomes the epic moment—not the everyday event
postponed in bars; or when you finally reach
the other side of the mountain
and all the paths lead down. As if
an ancient spell had been read backwards:
though what we'd seen—the burning cities
at our backs—had stopped us
in our tracks, a frozen chorus, colonnade
of salt, pillars like the wife of Lot,
the sight of her restored us
to ourselves. How else explain it? The way
she walked among us as we lined her path,
her gaze intent on us till we returned
her look, and then, like embers caught
in a sudden draft, our hope blazed up
again, the flush of blood crept up
reviving limbs . . . we laughed, embraced
and were so natural, so like old friends
picking up where we'd left off, it was as if
the interval of stone had gone
from memory, or it had never been.

But the cities *had* burned, the worst
had all been done, was, even now, being done
again—and yet, perhaps . . .

3

the one word not at our command: *perhaps*
to learn to live
in the dissolving grip of that green gaze,
put down the shield
emblazoned with the face
of Medusa, the mouth forever open
in a howl. The same face
Goya painted as the rifles were raised
and cocked, *Der Schrei* of Munch
at the vortex where one century of war plunged
into the next; the Pantheon
with its single vacant eye, Cyclops
cramming nations in his mouth—
an emptiness that nothing can assuage
creates its mirror image in
the gaping mouth, unfinished cry
as the head and the body are severed—the horror
on the hero's shield, the sound
of hoofs trampling the wind.

Reading the Bible Backwards

All around the altar, huge lianas
curled, unfurled the dark green
of their leaves to complement the red
of blood spilled there—a kind of Christmas
decoration, overhung with heavy vines
and over them, the stars.
When the angels came, messengers like birds
but with the oiled flesh of men, they hung
over the scene with smoldering swords,
splashing the world when they beat
their rain-soaked wings against the turning sky.

The child was bright in his basket
as a lemon, with a bitter smell from his wet
swaddling clothes. His mother bent
above him, singing a lullaby
in the liquid tongue invented
for the very young—short syllables
like dripping from an eave
mixed with the first big drops of rain
that fell, like tiny silver pears, from
the glistening fronds of palm. The three
who gathered there—old kings uncrowned:
the cockroach, condor and the leopard, lords
of the cracks below the ground, the mountain
pass and the grass-grown plain, were not
adorned, did not bear gifts, had not
come to adore; they were simply drawn
to gawk at this recurrent, awkward son
whom the wind had said would spell
the end of earth as it had been.

Somewhere north of this familiar scene
the polar caps were melting, the water was
advancing in its slow, relentless

lines, swallowing the old
landmarks, swelling the seas that pulled
the flowers and the great steel cities down.
The dolphins sport in the rising sea,
anemones wave their many arms like hair
on a drowned gorgon's head, her features
softened by the sea beyond all recognition.

On the desert's edge where the oasis dies
in a wash of sand, the sphinx seems to shift
on her haunches of stone, and the rain, as it runs down,
completes the ruin of her face. The Nile
merges with the sea, the waters rise
and drown the noise of earth. At the forest's
edge, where the child sleeps, the waters gather—
as if a hand were reaching for the curtain
to drop across the glowing, lit tableau.

When the waves closed over, completing the green
sweep of ocean, there was no time for mourning.
No final trump, no thunder to announce
the silent steal of waters; how soundlessly
it all went under: the little family
and the scene so easily mistaken
for an adoration. Above, more clouds poured in
and closed their ranks across the skies;
the angels, who had seemed so solid, turned
quicksilver in the rain.
                              Now, nothing but the wind
moves on the rain-pocked face
of the swollen waters, though far below
where giant squid lie hidden in shy tangles,
the whales, heavy-bodied as the angels,
their fins like vestiges of wings,
sing some mighty epic of their own—

a great day when the ships would all withdraw,
the harpoons fail of their aim, the land
dissolve into the waters, and they would swim
among the peaks of mountains, like eagles
of the deep, while far below them, the old
nightmares of earth would settle
into silt among the broken cities, the empty
basket of the child would float
abandoned in the seaweed until the work of water
unraveled it in filaments of straw,
till even that straw rotted
in the planetary thaw the whales prayed for,
sending their jets of water skyward
in the clear conviction they'd spill back
to ocean with their will accomplished
in the miracle of rain: *And the earth
was without form and void, and darkness
was upon the face of the deep. And
the Spirit moved upon the face of the waters.*

Miriam's Song

Death to the first-born sons, always—
the first fruits to the gods of men.
She had not meant it so, standing in the reeds
back then, the current tugging at her skirt
like hands, she had only meant to save
her little brother, Moses,
red-faced with rage when he was given
to the river. The long curve of the Nile
would keep their line, the promised land
around the bend. Years later
when the gray angel, like the smoke trail
of a dying comet, passed by the houses
with blood smeared over doorways,
Miriam, her head hot in her hands, wept
as the city swelled
with the wail of Egypt's women.
Then she straightened up, slowly plaited
her hair and wound it tight around her head,
drew her long white cloak with its deep blue threads
around her, went out to watch the river
where Osiris, in his golden funeral barge,
floated by forever . . .

as if in offering, she placed a basket on the river,
this time an empty one, without the precious cargo
of tomorrow. She watched it drift a little
from the shore. She threw one small stone in it,
then another, and another, till its weight
was too much for the water and it slowly turned
and sank. She watched the Nile gape and shudder,
then heal its own green skin. She went
to join the others, to leave one ruler
for another, one Egypt for the next.

Some nights you still can see her, by some river
where the willows hang, listening to the heavy tread
of armies, those sons once hidden dark
in baskets, and in her mind she sees her sister,
the black-eyed Pharaoh's daughter, lift the baby
like a gift from the brown flood waters
and take him home to save him, such a pretty
boy and so disarming, as his dimpled hands
reach up, his mouth already open
for the breast.

The Anabasis of Koré

Mother, she said rising
through the thawing earth, the opening
torn through stone and mud by her own descent

Mother, she said rising
through the first pale shoots of green, delicate
intruders—fragile, overlooked—
that pry open even the unforgiving
earth of Greece, the country whose dry air
we took for clarity
we who came from hazy Northern lands
wrapped in furs and mist, it was hard
to tell the hunter from the prey

Mother, she said, as she began to feel
the warm light of a Northern spring
on her shoulders, too white
from their sunless season in Hell
Mother, she said, it was I
who tired of the arid land of distinctions
the searing, inquisitorial light
of the Attic sun, who ate with such relish
the six sweet seeds wrapped in their wet, red flesh
who loved the damp corridors of Hell
where every drop that fell
from the dripping cavern walls was music

Nothing like your stony kingdom of thistles
where the sound of wind is like the scratching
of nails on slate, where mourning takes the form
of drought—the Greek summer when even the rivers
burn out, leaving the land scarred
with a cursive writing whose meaning
has dried with its ink. Only the oleanders
growing in the dry beds remind us, their pink

a pale echo of the deep red blossoms
on the pomegranate trees that crowd
the corridors of Hell, its rooms hung
in the lurid velvets of damnation—purple, gold
and burgundy, done up like a palace of decadent gods
on the eve of the Götterdämmerung
when the wine cups overflow until dawn
spills its crimson light
and a black sun rises, spider
in the cup of scarlet wine

Mother, it was I
picking white flowers that day in early spring
who shuddered at the dry rasp of wind
like an unfeeling, clinical hand on my skin
who became lost in a reverie of desire
until my hot dream split the ground
with a white slice of lightning
called up the dark chariot
with its gorgeous black horses, conjured up
the romantic figure in his black swirl of cape
like a storm rising in a Gothic landscape
to drag me out of your world

And it was I who wanted it all:
to be Queen of Hell and be innocent—
Persephone *and* Koré—who could resist
such a delicious duplicity? For it was I
who could not get enough of him
his green eyes and dark face a death
I only half understood, but wholly
desired. He so smug and aloof on his throne
in the great robes I had labored
to embellish, stitching with gold
a royal ikon, worth the soul's surrender.
But in my dreams, it was him I saw
soaked in his own blood, terribly wounded, dyeing
purple the garments of majesty, over and over.

And I remember with a shudder the first Mother, Gaia
drawing the iron from her own breast
sharpening the sickle, arming the son
against the father: Kronos to castrate Uranos, Zeus
to kill Kronos, spring after winter, world without end

In that dark time, tyrant blood flowed secretly
into the gleaming black waters of Hell
slowly returning my own power
with which I had endowed him, helping him keep us all
in the dark, down there where no man
held us in thrall, for Death is
nobody, only the absolute
zero in vanity's jar, the one I gave Psyche
that promised beauty but gave her instead
ignorance and deep sleep

Yes, Mother, it was I who called out to you
so long ago, terrified of my own desire, hating
to be carried away, afraid to leave
or to stay—that cry was my old self parting
leaving open the way of return.
So you would always have come for me
too late, when I no longer belong to your kingdom
nor to that other below

Saying that she turned away
from her whose veil the wind
lifted, whose limbs the sun shone
through, whose form held its outline
a moment, a dandelion's ghost of down
one puff of wind enough
to disperse it—just a flurry of dust
in the sunlight, or, in the wind-stirred air
a sudden white fury of seeds

Minor Epic

The rock where the sword was stuck—
a silver cross that topped the granite,
its business end discreetly buried,
waiting to be hauled out
by a youth, sweet and full of promise
as only legends make them—holds nothing now
but an empty shaft of stone, as vacant
as the dream that the best would rule
when only the worst would want to . . .

the lake is wise to this, so when
King Arthur, once more dying, tosses in
Excalibur, the arm—as slender and as silver
as a trout—will not be there to catch it,
a feudal hope as broken as
the surface with its spreading rings
to mark the spot the sword has entered
deep, impassive blue. They're sending
divers, rubber-suited and pursued
by bubbles, their anxious faces pressed
to glass, searching for the sword
the lake has taken to its heart
that they will never find
in the mud and murk and weeds
down there, its silver blade impaled
in the lady, neatly nailed
to the bottom of the lake.

Today they're hauling up the Mary Rose
from the bottom of the channel, her hold
stuffed with bric-a-brac and bones
of the brave gentlemen of Henry Eight
who took time out from eating
his stupendous roasts to sail
against the French, or rather, watched
from his royal bluff as the Mary Rose,

spread-eagled under men and armor, rolled over,
sank like a diving duck in search of dinner
and stayed below for centuries, a spectral
Tudor country week-end party
with its grinning guests. The Prince
of Wales watches as the carcass
lifts above the channel, dripping
things historic—a cable snaps, but the hull
is saved with only a shattered
timber, cannons fire their salute
from a nearby castle, the hulk
is swung on board and brought to shore,
disarmed and rotten, to the cheers
of a little crowd standing
under water, umbrellas raised
beneath the sovereign English rain.

Desert Parable

Miles above them, miles below—
nothing but the heat-stunned air
the hum of insects hovering close
to the tenacious brush that clung
to the canyon wall, the canyon that had been
dry as far back as even the Grandfathers
could remember. Some said the earth
had swallowed the river back, others
that the sky had picked the canyon dry,
hid the river in white sacks
of cloud and carried it to where
the grazing isn't bitter.

She knew the footholds on the cliff
by heart. By day or night, she could pick
her way straight up or down the nicks
cut in the vertical stone. Custom was the purchase
on that rock—only tribal feet could find
their hold and climb the sheer face down
to the pueblo, tucked in the hollow
time had dug in the sandstone wall.
It was the same with hands—the pattern
that your fingers knew, the blankets
woven in the same strict stitch, the zigzag
like the distant lightning flash, until
even in the dark, you could pull the wool across
the tight-strung loom. But she was too restless
to sit with the women and weave; her mind
wandered to another place where the rains fell
thick and sudden like your hair when the combs
are pulled, the teeth of bone let go. And where
the arrows of the sun were broken
by the leaves. Her fingers, following her mind,
lost their place on the taut strings,

tied knots and broke the even rhythms
of the old design. At night, she often called out
in her sleep; by day, picked fights
at the slightest provocation. When the peace
of evening settled on the tribe, her lungs
closed like a fist, she couldn't
breathe; a dark prayer rose
from her—smoke pouring
from a kiva-hole
toward heaven.

At last they drove her from the pueblo
up the sheer cliff to the waiting sky.

By night the men filled in
two of the toe-holds, moved
them slightly to the right
so if she tried to climb back
to the village, she would fall
into the endless canyon
of the sky; the buzzards would pick
her bones till they glistened white
as stars. The tribe went back
about its tasks, stolid,
reassured. "She didn't know,"
the old ones said,
"the pueblo is the world."

For the first time that night she slept
without the covering ledge
without the even breathing of the others
in her ears . . .

                just the boundless dark

uninhabited by everything but light

          that drew her till she whirled among the stars
                a pot turned on the great wheel of the sky
until
          in all that burning night

          her own clay seemed to shatter   she felt

a singing in her veins like water   a rush
          of silver that poured out like rain

                and she was lost among

          the galaxies—squash blossoms
               silver   like the necklace of her mother but
               without its weight   so light   it was

          quicksilver   thistledown
               a gleaming river of spilled milk   perhaps

     a tongue, a tide of light
                    lapping at the shores
                              those farther shores
                                        than night

Time Out of Mind

. . . it becomes exceedingly difficult to grasp the continuity between normal existence and the hour at which hell starts, on the city square when the Germans begin the deportations, or . . . wherever . . .
—George Steiner

It begins in the garret of a tower
the old crone humming at her spinning
turning the wheel like a planet,
like a world. Outside her window, cut
high in the turret wall, the fields stretch out
in emerald lawn, sewn with pearls
of sheep—distant, precious, picturesque
as illustrations in an antique book.
She grows distracted; her foot
is weary on the treadle—she is merely
what we all become. (Because of that
she's sometimes taken, in the ancient tales,
for fate.) Her eyes, a faded blue, stare out
into that distance deep within
where all the stories start.

Across the fields, where memory leads
as a shepherdess her sheep, a young girl
walks, her mind a bright embroidery
of dreams—as beautiful as it is thin,
worn almost out by time. And where the moon is
stitched, the fabric's torn, the day beyond
comes through. She tries to pull
the too thin fabric back, to wind
the world again in fable. Her head
is a burden to her neck, a blossom
grown too heavy for its stem. The light
is too intense for her new eyes; she sees
a partly opened door, goes in, climbs
up the spiral staircase hewn of stone,
drawn by the strange humming of the wheel.

Remember how it went? How she, alarmed
at first, is taken in, sits down where the crone
had sat and takes the spindle up, then
pricks her finger—one dark drop of red
begins to spread until the world is drenched
in it, as if she'd grown a red lens
on her eyes, the way the world looks to a snake
for whom the heat of things is visible,
its fire no guessed-at thing.

Years pass. Winter
following winter, the snow drifts down.

The station is crowded with travelers
though the expression that they wear, and the way
they hold their children to them, shows
this is no ordinary trip. The city burns
behind them; they file on the train; the sky
is a strange sulphuric gray, gray faces,
gray smoke that pours out from the wheels
of the train; it is, all of it, gray . . .
so many to be dead, the damned, the long lines
of the hopeless who don't believe
what they must know is coming—Treblinka's
painted clock says three, forever three. Time
and the terrible retelling have turned it
to a shadow play—then, an etching, black and white
and gray in a German edition of Dante.
Sleep spared her this; unaware,
she couldn't know how memory had grown
numb, the tongue as gray and heavy
as wet cement where nothing left
the mute print of its thumb.

When she wakes, her hair is white. It is no
prince who brings her back, but sun
slanting through the frame to light the room—

the long threads cut and scattered on the floor,
the broken spinning wheel, her own hands
idle in her lap. It wasn't sleep, then, claimed the years
but the undoing of a dream. In the corner
of her eye, she sees the spider, black and busy,
shaping its silk to catch the glinting rays
of sun, fine silver to gather dust.
The old woman gets up, as if to shrug off
the idea of fate; now she knows
we come after the dream, the one that made
the nightmare journey real. And that it's time
to take the long flight of stone steps
down, the spiral leading out—to pastures
greener than the fabled fields, uneven, springy
to the foot. She doesn't hurry as she moves
among the grazing sheep as yet unshorn
nor does she shield her eyes against
the brilliant light, letting them fill, letting
the tears run down her face, streams
unloosed by spring, the most
that sun could make
of so many winters, so much snow.

Sarah's Choice

A little late rain
the desert in the beauty of its winter
bloom, the cactus ablaze
with yellow flowers that glow
even at night in the reflected light
of moon and the shattered crystal of sand
when time was so new
that God still walked
among the tents, leaving no prints
in the sand, but a brand burned into
the heart—on such a night
it must have been, although
it is not written in the Book
how God spoke to Sarah
what he demanded of her
how many questions came of it
how a certain faith was
fractured, as a stone is split
by its own fault, a climate of extremes
and one last drastic change
in the temperature.

"Go!" said the Voice. "Take your son,
your only son, whom you love,
take him to the mountain, bind him
and make of him a burnt offering."
Now Isaac was the son of Sarah's age,
a gift, so she thought, from God. And how
could he ask her even to imagine such a thing—
to take the knife
of the butcher and thrust it
into such a trusting heart, then
light the pyre on which tomorrow burns.
What fear could be more holy
than the fear of *that?*

"Go!" said the Voice, Authority's own.
    And Sarah rose to her feet, stepped out
    of the tent of Abraham to stand between
    the desert and the distant sky, holding its stars
    like tears it was too cold to shed.
    Perhaps she was afraid the firmament
    would shudder and give way, crushing her
    like a line of ants who, watching
    the ants ahead marching safe under the arch,
    are suddenly smashed by the heel
    they never suspected. For Sarah,
    with her desert-dwelling mind, could
    see the grander scale in which the heel
    might simply be the underside of some Divine
    intention. On such a scale, what is
    a human son? So there she stood, absurd
    in the cosmic scene, an old woman bent
    as a question mark, a mote in the eye
    of God. And then it was that Sarah spoke
    in a soft voice, a speech
    the canon does not record.

"No," said Sarah to the Voice.   *The*
"I will not be chosen. Nor shall my son—   *teachings*
    if I can help it. You have promised Abraham,   *of Sarah*
    through this boy, a great nation. So either
    this sacrifice is sham, or else it is a sin.
    Shame," she said, for such is the presumption
    of mothers, "for thinking me a fool,
    for asking such a thing. You must have known
    I would choose Isaac. What use have I
    for History—an arrow already bent
    when it is fired from the bow?"

Saying that, Sarah went into the tent
    and found her restless son awake, as if
    he'd grown aware of the narrow bed in which he lay.

And Sarah spoke out of the silence
she had herself created, or that had been there
all along. "Tomorrow you will be
a man. Tonight, then, I must tell you
the little that I know. You can be chosen
or you can choose. Not both.

The voice of the prophet grows shrill.
He will read even defeat as a sign
of distinction, until pain itself
becomes holy. In that day, how shall we tell
the victims from the saints,
the torturers from the agents of God?"

"But mother," said Isaac, "if we were not God's
chosen people, what then should we be? I am afraid
of being nothing." And Sarah laughed.

Then she reached out her hand. "Isaac,
I am going now, before Abraham awakes, before
the sun, to find Hagar the Egyptian and her son
whom I cast out, drunk on pride,
God's promises, the seed of Abraham
in my own late-blooming loins."

The
unbinding
of Isaac

"But Ishmael," said Isaac, "how should I greet him?"
"As you greet yourself," she said, "when you bend
over the well to draw water and see your image,
not knowing it reversed. You must know your brother
now, or you will see your own face looking back
the day you're at each other's throats."

She wrapped herself in a thick dark cloak
against the desert's enmity, and tying up
her stylus, bowl, some dates, a gourd
for water—she swung her bundle on her back,
reached out once more toward Isaac.

23

"It's time," she said. "Choose now."

"But what will happen if we go?" the boy
 Isaac asked. "I don't know," Sarah said
"But it is written   what will happen   if you stay."

II Companions

Postscript

—to Maxine Kumin

Dear Max. I call you that because
two syllables are too much for the sharp
pain your poems cause, the ache
between the shoulder blades, from
what the older centuries called
heart. You're right
and there is something you can do, I can't:
say "I" and "love" and "gone" and
cut it right, neat as a split cord of wood,
the exact heft of the axe,
the straight, swift stroke.

Last week I tried to saw
a dead branch off the firethorn, and halfway
through I had to stop, not knowing
what I'd do when the damn thing started
falling . . . standing there, imagining
how it would pull down the power lines,
the wires for the phone, the healthy branch
below, and then, as it tore down
through all the wreckage of those lines
and ruined garden, it would hit me,
its thorns tear through my scalp,
put out my eyes and leave me bleeding
for the neighbors to discover. This sad
and total inability to cut
a simple branch down from the tree
when it was dead a year, this image
like some cheap disaster
film, makes me afraid
of scissors and of saw, of lighting fires,
of using "I," for fear I'll start
some mad striptease of art, tell all,
embarrass everyone, even the dog

and bring the gossip hounds to sniff
the ruins, the mess I made of it all,
like some baroque explosion in a clean
well-lighted room, and then climb out
onto the windowsill and hoot and
hoot like some demented owl, her feathers
damp from her own rain of tears,
trying to reel back the years—
and not the ones behind, that any fool
would not repeat—but those ahead
that speed up like a train
whose rails I'm tied to
like some poor, abandoned heroine
in a film that everyone is in
so no one wants to see it
over. And yet when you, refusing
both amnesia and the comfort of a myth
can talk as straight as one might
hold a saw to get the dead branch down,
somehow, you save the tree.

While I can't face
the amputation of a branch without
the towers of Troy beginning to go over
like Humpty Dumpty toppling through the years,
his scattered bits the Hittites, the Sumerians,
the Greeks, the Romans (row on row on row),
the French in the deep freeze of the Russian
snow, and don't forget the Jews, the Congolese,
the British Empire shrinking to
tin soldiers on the counterpane
and next America and all that now lives
with her, and then the planet like
a candle sputters out, and the sun
begins to fail in the heavens
and the cold sky fills
with an avalanche of angels, overweight,
falling through their feathers, with
burning hair like figures out of Blake,

and the planets break
their orbits and collide, the firmament
begins to crack and those old waters
that the Fathers said lay just beyond it
pour through the cracks in torrents,
close over everything (except this sonorous
voice-over, this announcer, who seems
to live out universal floods
and still not skip a beat, or miss
a comma)—

       you see, I find myself
in a false position, and wish
some sanity would overtake me, like
Don Quijote unhorsed by the Knight
of Mirrors, and just say: dear,
could you just manage
to pull yourself together, take out
the trash and understand the universal
crash is not your business; your flight
from simply stating, from talking straight
as Max, is not being able
to do what Albrecht Dürer did
in just one simple drawing
in his notebook, shortly
before his own untimely death (for
whose death is not untimely?).
It was a portrait of himself, a naked man,
his right arm bent and pointing
at his middle, and written there
below it, just one line,
no easier in German:
"Here, it hurts."

Going the Rounds

—for Dr. Janet Abrahm

The doctor goes her rounds again—
the trouble is the stagnant air, the passive
patients in their beds, as bulbs
too long in the earth soften
from too many rains and the silt
left by flood after flood, the mulch overfed
by the passage overhead of too many
birds, whose droppings bristle with seed
like pomegranates, or grenades.
It's a bad season for coaxing health
from the stew of earth, the flood plain
of a sea-level life, whose incessant storms
have put their wet hands on the soil,
worked it like a mad potter
who has forgotten the shape of things
to come or even the simple round
of clay to hold the moment in.

The shoes of the doctor slip, then stick
in the ooze; even the sun is sickly,
barely more than a mustard glow
in the heavy murk. What balm could heal
the fetors of this marsh, could speed
the weak, insistent pulse she takes
in passing, raising here and there a pallid
wrist, limp, from the litter of fallen
things? Or stop the calling for a cure,
the mud that drags her down?

The numbers waiting to be treated seem
to grow, filling the world like a wet woods
with mushrooms, the pale heads pushing
through the damp loam, the cries muffled
in the hanging moss, the veils of mist.
She reaches for the only solid thing

in sight, a black branch hanging over
the unreflective swamp, where mud and water
won't sort out, and the sponge
of soil drinks everything in.
She feels her way along the strong, abrasive branch,
the earth sucking at her feet, her prints
turning, behind her, into pools of ink . . .
until she feels at last the round
bole of the oak, its rough bark
a balm against her cheek, the hard trunk
a solace to her arms, dark axis
in a world grown indistinct. Bracing
her feet on the swell of the roots, then
on the bole, she begins to climb
finding footholds in the little ledges
of the bark, the forks
of the branches spreading out and up,
the ladder of the limbs—
till, all at once, she breaks out
into brightness, where the air is fresh
and the warming rays of sun are
like a laying on of hands. She rests
in the brilliant air above the grey swirl
of cloud, hears the clear call of birds, poised
on the tip end of the twigs, their flight
imminent—while she clings there, unable
to climb higher, unwilling to climb
down, perched in that temporary
nest between the realms
where, if the weather holds, something
may hatch. She remembers then

the hunger
of all things newly born.
She sighs, begins
the long climb down
to go on with her rounds
moving through the gloom she must dispel

carrying the memory of the sun
swinging in her head
like a lantern in a storm—
its beam lancing the dark.

Homage to the River

—and to Emily Grosholz

The mind moves away
from in front of the mind, graceful,
swaying in the reeds that grow slantwise,
tangent to the wind, a weathervane
that's light enough to swing
with the slightest air, and where
we walked, the grass springs
back, our step erased, and where
we left our watermark, cut clean
with oar and straining back
and the mind that drove them on—wave
merged with wave, the long division gone.
Here, the river is all
indolence and clear decision as it sings
its own sweet cadence out, moves swifter
as it sweeps the curves, geometry
lost in a Chinese eye that never cared
to find triangles in the hills nor fix
a vanishing point for a single, ruling eye
but saw instead the hills as shadow's flesh
melting into cloud, and clouds as heaven breathing
in the stream, and out, to find the earth again
as rain, and mist the marriage veil
of those great dancing partners, yin and yang,
and there beside the stream, someone
almost lost in the shore's tall grass, small
as a figure in a vast unrolling scroll
by a master's hand, the river's bright calligrapher
a writing changing shape with all it saw.

Though she regret she can't quite
"carry out the spring," nor enter water
in that lovely loss the sages sing, I say

to stay is homage too, to hold your ground
a kind of prayer, as reeds
adorn the edge of things, and bending
in the moving air, give their own reflection up
to the passing stream—bowing
in the oldest human gesture of respect.

Tucson Gardens

—on the Arizona photographs of William Larson

The wagon trails stopped here, ditched
at the desert's edge. Fish left this ocean
long ago to sand. Here only the wind speaks
Spanish, and, at the edge of town, the ghosts
of conquistadors blow, light as tumbleweed
across dry ground. The green here is sad,
it lives on artificial rain, sprinklers and
long vinyl snakes, the hoses of the human host—
fence-builder, who answers the tangle of dry
vine, the palm's shaggy explosion of fronds,
the riot of the nerves, the intricate curves
of the wild—with the plumb line,
the cube of cement, the grid of the mind.

Our time, held still in the cool gaze of the lens,
a chemical fix, the shutter poised
under your finger like a trigger—
nothing moves. This is the suburb,
stubborn, the gardens of us temporary gods.
Out there, the mountains are a line
drawn on a graph, a record
of the rise and fall
of unrecorded time.

There is desert out there, pal,
and here, the placid battle lines are drawn—
chain links, trellis and the picket fence
make their last stand. The hand, if it were
freed, if it reached out and touched,
would bleed, the cactus bristling
like a porcupine, the garden of thorns,
the cypress like the feathers
of dead Indians, guardians
at the edge of open land.

But what most strongly haunts this place
is us, a strange nostalgia
for the present.
How else explain the careful emptiness,
the unkempt cultivation of a place
both occupied, deserted—abandoned
Arizona of the heart, where
we are missing
in the middle of our lives.
How else explain, in a place so dry,
the soft watercolor wash of sky,
the pale green, as if we thinned
our palette with our tears.
How else explain the quality of light
that turns the otherwise familiar scene
to the hand-tinted postcards of a dream,
a gentler time, pasted in an album
on a shelf. Here, where the west begins
to end—regret, the empty
garden seat, the yucca
like a dried bouquet
of bayonets, the thorny hedge
defends the secret houses
where we hide, wounded birds
who dream of flight
alone and exiled
in our nests.

The American Sublime: Robert Penn Warren

High in the mountain pass, tucked in a crevice
of stone, the eagle's nest throbs
with its naked young, open-mouthed and crying
to be fed. The eagle soars, the voice
of the wind in the highest pines
doesn't whine; it sounds,
to a human ear, like sobbing.

Old man, we say you're too rhetorical and
too sublime, as if an eagle when it spread
wide wings and rode the cold wind
down the mountain pass, its great yellow eye
wide open, could be other than it is.

Below, deep in the years, a boy
and his husky, *Sila,* a ruin of stonework,
a blank sheet of snow: there
for the billionth time since the earth
begat, and the cells moved in their unknowing,
mindful way toward flesh and fur, the dog
leaped at the doe's throat and the snow
blossomed red as a bridal
sheet—the doe torn, the dog
docile again, stained crimson
on its silver muzzle, confused
by the pain on its master's face, himself
armed for the kill. And you, that boy
grown old, the taste of blood
still fresh from the knife that cut short
the death throes of the deer, the blood still
warm on the blade after so many years, unable
to make it right, to make it fit without
the bite of the saw-wheel, tooth on tooth, turning
as the planet turns, the sun staining the sky
with red, the snow falling again
in useless white denial.

37

                    We, who say the word
ecology as if it were God, accuse you
of the orator's sin, you
who looked long and long into the cold
blue eyes of the husky and
the warm brown eyes of the doe—
and wept, and cried out . . . what words
without the rhetorical sweep
like the wide-open wings of the eagle
riding the cold current at the top of the pass
could do it justice, this world
without justice or help
for the heart, beating
like the helpless young in their nest
crying for the sky-driven beak, seeing, at last,
the great bird coming like love
down over them, bringing death in its beak
to comfort them, and the huge darkness
of itself, like love, for cover
against the cold galactic night.

The Autumn of the Poets

(Variation on the French of Layla Ahsan)

The way the first freeze
breaks the glass, with the barest
silver sprinkle of sound
crystal shatters, spills
the sun it held all summer—

so autumn breaks the spellbound heart
of that enchanted summer when, for days,
it was always noon, the sun
swallowing back the shadows

      it was that stricken   that still
         the bright composure
            of the unsuspecting

we'd spent the idle August days
its interval of stunned light
manning the battlements of the castle
every stone a denial, every stair
another twisted step toward
dream, every arrow sharpened, poison-barbed
poised at the walls, bows drawn, the answer
to a siege, a mighty host
of doubts

we had the sea surrounded, nailed
up the sun—there wasn't a thing
not under our spell, love
it was all of it ours
we were ourselves the harbor & the sail
cut from the horizon's blue, the cry
from the crow's nest, the answering shout
from the shore.
The spinning wrecks were nothing
to do with us.

Though all the time the fading leaves
were whispering
like conspirators
and in the silence after
in profound silence
winter crouches
approaches now from every side
slower & slower as it nears
as if the walls we built
to keep cold out
were slowly
closing
in

"He was the whitest white man
I had ever met"

—for Vernon Young, in memoriam

Gaunt, English parson in his mien;
in manner, imperious; his clothes
an elegance gone slightly seedy, out of date
as had his looks—he had an antique frame
and a disease that made his bones as brittle
as his hopes. Disappointed, spiteful,
querulous, allergic to the ruder forms
of life, the energy of urban streets
chilled further the cold fury of his
injured pride. He seemed the haunted ruin
of an imperial idea, a run-down dream
of gallantry and art that
cheerfully forced half the world
to its design, an Oriental carpet for the feet
of a royal progess, souls pressed
into its service to support a style,
like ebon statues, the tapers burning
on their heads, a crown of light to hold at bay
the waiting night—
we had a bitter fight about all that.

And yet, for all the tawdry grandeur,
snobbery, the spider in the cup he drank
and must have seen—there was
a boyish sweetness that broke out
as sun does when a sudden gust
opens a sky that was, for days,
a solid lid of iron grey—
a sudden, sumptuous glow whenever he spoke
of poetry, of Nature, a great scene in a film—
anything beautifully made or done
tuned to the gut strings of the soul

might strike him like that sun—and all of him
alight, who was redeemed
a moment in the circle of that lucid warmth—
the "room without corners" he dreamed.

And who shall hymn the lonely, fragile
heart that lives inside
the sometime misanthrope,
a childhood spoiled somehow,
its perfect scene: no memory
but hope embalmed, like the precious world
in the paperweight that, shaken, fills with snow,
the moment that he'd waited for, how many
afternoons? Watching the sun
at last break through the enduring
English clouds and pick out objects
one by one—a wrought iron chair, a bit
of hedge, he might have thought: but one more
shift of cloud, the sun will rest on me.

Too much solitude and dark, the twenty
Swedish winters that he stayed, dark
except for the books he loved and the flickering
square of the movie screen; he sealed
the world away from him
with a solid shield of solipsistic
chill. And like the walrus that navigates
below the ice of northern seas, and when in need
of air comes up, hurls his full weight against
the solid ceiling of the ice, breaks through
to light and oxygen—one year he finds himself
too old to break the icy firmament
through which the sun but feebly bends its rays,
and throws and throws himself against
the ice but lacks the strength
to open it and reach the light, and so succumbs
to the same North Sea where he was spawned.

*   *   *

That night I'd left him
in intensive care, bleeding his life away;
the web was torn and no transfusion now
could slow the red tide of his going.
He looked at me, and shook his head.
Later, as I lay sleepless, his helpless
suffering tossing in my mind, he all at once
appeared, there in the room, no dream,
dressed jauntily, as for an Alpine stroll.
He wore, as I recall, a Tyrol hat with a feather
iridescent in the light that came in with him,
and he was smiling, utterly at ease.
He walked a little distance off, and waved.
I slept then, almost the "sweet and dreamless
sleep" of the blest. At dawn
I called the hospital. He was gone.

        *   *   *

It was a bonny summer day
under the sun's clear sign
when we few friends took his ashes down
to the river, giving him up to the current's slide.
The ashes hung for a startled moment
before they fell—a genie sudden in the sunlit air,
giving off a kind of smoke, a plume of dust
infused with light, and fuming
like the very life.

"Never Apologize for Poetry"

—for my students

Despite the times, the cursèd spite
there is still music
in the leaves and magic in the cunning
spiral of a snail, and falling water
with its lovely, ruinous cascade of sound,
all this that beggars speech and yet
gives tongue. And when we say, "I, too, hate
poetry," it is not modesty forbids
the brag of art, but this abundant
wily earth our words must fail. Yet
in this union with the word, the long reach
of our little minds that compass
galaxies and quail before the corners
of a room at night, can still
ignite what otherwise might just go
   darkly
      on
as a fox deep in the hedgerow
brings its eyes to light
the otherwise too blank a green
and gazing out, gives that strange
brilliance to the dark luxuriance of leaves—
though here the trope must fail before
the fox, who suddenly gets up, swerves out
of our conceit to go its own
unhuman way, and yet the last
red blaze of tail, defiant plume
that waves off in the closing grass, turns back
into an emblem of our concealment,
red flag to warn the others off, meanwhile
our eyes will go on burning, stay
when all the world goes on its accidental
artful way—a double vision
bright inside the hedge, nature
given memory and pause . . .

as sun pays homage to the solid world
by laying shadows at its feet, as sky
lies looking up from the reflecting ponds
and clouds rest easily among
the lily pads, the sky and water, blue
and green, are so at one
that those two realms they say the gods
divided at the start, are mixed again
along these shaded paths, so far
from war, where leaves command
their ancient speech and falling water
telling its passage in the hand
has its own cool blue renewed
by touching us, the spell is cast
and joyful and assured
of our defeat, we spell it back
(*adieu*) into anotherhand.

"Into the Distance Where All Things Reverse and Touch"

—for Mary and Phoebe

She pressed her head against the screen
until the scene bowed out, as a player
leaves the stage when the lights come up
in the house and the forest dims
that had been mad with green, light
rippled, woven in the way that will defeat
geometries, heroic lines that stand
like soldiers in formation, a phalanx
for a pyramid, the parallels incessant.
She pulls back from the mediating screen
that squares the air minutely, keeps
the insects out (though she can hear them
humming); the metal had set the print
of little squares on the tight-stretched
skin of her forehead. The room was bare
and cool, lit from inside against
the tree-hung shade: the oak
rectangle of the bench, pearls
in the dish where berries might have been,
a shell lifting its pink ear
on the gray grain of the table.

The window squares begin to fade and soften.
Like striking some exact equation
from a line, she switches off the overhead
to watch the daylight changing.
Outside, a ground mist rising, the outlines
blur, the twilight opens like a violet.
As the sun, far out at sea, grows close
to the horizon, its perfect circle
starts to bulge a little, as if
it felt the weight
of atmosphere,

a gentle pressure
on the eye
as what obscures the boundaries
delights some other sense
the inner eye obeys. As the sun
sinks into ocean,
suffusing everything
with light-filled water,
unhinged by wind
the screen door swings out
at a crazy angle—look,
the new moon rising!
She reaches up and cups it
in her hands—the distance nears:
all things reverse and touch.

Two Pairs of Eyes

—for Leah Kosh

Your eyes are dark and luminous and
mine are not-quite blue or green, depending
on the weather. We alter what we see: you
have the lunar eye and make an opalescent world
of mica chips, translucent fossil wings,
while I, born under the sign of sun, must seek
the glow of light through moving scrims
of gnat-wing, dragonfly. You love the gold leaf
of Byzantium, the sheen of peacock feathers;
I, the autumn sun, gold filtered
through the blazing copper beech.

You turn the snow to silver like the moon
and I regard it with the eye of sun, until
it slips away and swells the rivers.
You paint the stones across the stream
fot footing; I always slip
on the slick ones furred with moss
and slide the way a trout does
into shadows. Your ferns are like those pressed
by glaciers into rock, the permanent lace
earth wears beneath her changing skirts
of green. And I, as changeable as dust
on summer paths when the wind lifts it,
will shift the scales of time until
the ferns are huge as trees again and stir
the air with delicate green oars
as if the air were water.

You love blood-red enamel curled inside
the lips of conch, the claws that curve
like new moons at the tips of paws,
the deep luxuriance of fur, the violet impasto
of a royal bruise, the pearls that hatch

from parted lips, and marble eggs licked smooth
by the Aegean, the teeth inside a rose
that tears us with its beauty. And I,
why do I fear these relics with a holy fear?

For while shells build the glory of
a coral reef, I feel the crumbling
sand beneath my feet, torn out by tide.
I send what shells I find to you, dear friend
and astral eye, I who cannot read the bones
nor prophesy. These mysteries are not mine.
I gather shells for you, for love
but as I do, I cry—for what art cannot do,
no more can I; I turn and watch the tide.
It moves the shells in the glitter of the foam
almost, almost I say
as if they were alive.

III Lamentations

There Are Such Mornings

Though the difference between man and the other animals is enormous, yet one may say reasonably that it is little less than the difference among men themselves.

—Galileo Galilei

Sometimes you wake at night
when the street lamps throw
their sodium glare across the sheets
wake to the sound of the murdered dead
tramping through your room and through
your head, and finding neither reason
nor excuse, nor balm to place
on this torn wound, the world
you turn the light on by your bed
and read to still your soul
or sometimes, helpless, weep
and through the curtain of your grief
move to a fresh exhaustion
into a room that's quiet, cool
where you can sleep
at last, can sleep

and wake into that room as to a given
a place like some old-fashioned, simple heaven
where any dawn is Eden, a paradise
like Botticelli's, the French doors always open
to the shaded avenues of green
where figures dressed in saffron and in rose
a choreography of floating, fluted
gowns, feet so lively underneath
they barely brush the ground,
their voices soft as pastel strokes
on the bright blue air, they move, easy
knowing the way, along an avenue of lawn
half-lit through leaves, leisurely winding down
to the ever-breaking sea . . . a breezy *paradiso*

before Savonarola
let the Angel at the gate into the garden
brought Hell back to morning
the gentle Botticelli
a sleepwalker
suddenly awakened in the dawn
to a burning house
the sweet children
of his brush
put to the flaming sword

Beauty and the Beast

Her fur new-licked, the whitetail fawn
peers wide-eyed through the screen
of field grass, her ears outspread
to catch the slightest sound. Even asleep,
her ears are pricked and ready, as if
to catch intruders in her dreams.
But breathe her name, she's gone.

"These things in which we have seen
ourselves and spoken" turn from us now;
even the rocks, in which we glimpsed
enduring things, obscure themselves,
perhaps deliberately, in mist.
As deer, when caged in zoos or
put to other abstract uses,
lose their thick plush of russet
brown, the wetness of their
noses, their special way of stopping
at a sound—so when we fling our net
of thought, the living silver
of the ocean clots. To what
pass have we come, when hope
is no more than desire
to share in their oblivion,
when what seemed brute and dumb
till we had loaned it beauty's
tongue, seems now as eloquent
as silent heaven?

We, who burned our brand
into the uncomplaining flank
of the creation, begin to hope
for what may yet survive us . . .

and as the animals grow
smaller, moving off into a blue, inhuman
distance, we dare not call out
after them: "Good luck!"
for fear our best meant words, straight
from the heart, will follow them
as they depart, and curse them.

The Last Man
—for Vivian

Here, in our familiar streets, the day
is brisk with winter's business.
The reassuring rows of brick façades,
litter baskets overflowing
with the harvest of the streets
and, when the light turns, the people
move in unison, the cars miraculously
slide to a stop, no one is killed,
the streets, for some reason, do not
show the blood that is pouring
like a tide, on other shores.

      Martinez, the last peasant left alive
      in his village, refuses to run, hopes
      that God, *El Salvador,*
        will let him get the harvest in.
    "Can a fish live out of water?" he says
      for why he stays, and weeds
      another row, ignoring the fins
      of sharks that push up
      through the furrows.

Here, it is said, we live
in the belly of the beast. Ahab sits
forever at the helm, his skin
white wax, an effigy. The whale carries
him, lashed to its side by the ropes
from his own harpoon. His eyes
are dead. His ivory leg
juts from the flank of Leviathan
like a useless tooth.

One more time, the little sail appears
a cloud forms, an old ikon for mercy
turned up in a dusty corner
of the sky, preparing rain
for the parched land, Rachel
weeping for her children. "Can a fish
live out of water?" he asks
and the rain answers, in Spanish,
manitas de plata
little hands of silver on his brow.

Colloquy with Medea

(Variation on the Spanish of Inés Azar)

Some day, Medea,
the messengers will arrive
bringing news of a horror
more general than your own,
of a century that engendered
only a blind child, unable
to catch its breath
between the fumes of a gas so sweet
it is almost floral and
the cold, odorless, air-conditioned
space of madness—
a child to whom dreams were denied:
the wrath of Achilles,
the reverent deceits of Odysseus,
the passion of Medea
who loves and forgives
nothing.

The news will arrive
that now
the serene indifference of your gods
the difficult virtue of your heroes
the great weight of beauty and error
matter to no one
and all that made you
as you were, desperate and implacable,
concerns no one,
being merely the absolute affront.

They will tell you more.
They will drag you by the hand
through the alleys and margins,
up the back stairs of history, until
you arrive at the precise passage,

the impeccable line that proves
what was real is nothing.
They will shout in your ear
that you are scarcely a name
in a dead language; that a Greek,
sparing of words, spectral
as you, dreamed you
for the punishment and glory
of other ghosts,
a shade among shadows.

And you, who know it now,
who all along knew it,
you will smile almost with humility,
observing, briefly, the forms
of resignation. Then, you will tear your breast
where the heart beats in a desert of sand.
And you will lift in your hand
an ancient book, the one where it is written
that your gods knew of a time so distant
that the moon was a cradle of steel,
a machete that swung
among stars, murdering
the tongues of men.
That your gods knew it.
And that, in their piety,
they forgot.

Infection in the Ear

Under the quiet that is not calm
but its sad counterfeit, the dulled,
a silence that would once have seemed
unearthly, before we knew what earthly was,
is merely our last refuge here,
for we were deafened by too many screams,
the word for scream itself became
unseemly, an overstated thing to be
crossed out of poems—even in dreams
the tongue must move in silence, cautious,
like a swimmer underwater in the dark,
for only the deaf ear can discern
in the dull, resisting air
what moves like distant thunder underneath:
the barely audible, the underbeat.

Is it the still enduring heart?
Or is it, from a country closer
than comfort, the hollow boom of guns
making a fretwork out of solid walls
where the maimed and newly dead
cannot be heard inside their ruined homes
because the ear can bear no more?
This infection of our inward ear, no
penicillin touches nor can cure;
it is the earthly last
defense, tuning out atrocity,
so that what is, and so might be, can hear
itself and keep, though unaccompanied,
the underbeat—the muffled bass that once
played under melody, and now, plays on, alone—
a foot on the treadle of a loom
in a deserted room, shades drawn
against the massacre of light.

As Far As It Goes, and Back

Tearing through the lovely landscape
of Honshu—its brief perfections—the bullet
train cutting them short,
boring through mountain after mountain,
black shaft driven
through the deep volcanic night
then breaking out, for a held breath
into the sun, a flash of green fields
flooded with water, half-filled with sky—
then back to the black again.

Those green, happy valleys
out of a child's book, like bright
spaces between the words in a sentence
whose meaning is dark—tunnel
after tunnel, all I can see of the heart
of Japan, except for the brief blaze
of green against the glass—those tall young
mountains in their pointed sorcerers' hats
of tufted green velvet, the nestled farms,
each roof with its curling lift
of wings at the outer edge, ready
at the first tremor of earth
to fly . . . how easily it all
slips by, slips back

to a bright memory,
a never-never land, seen only
as lost children see, wandering
in time, the sudden reflection
of a mother in the mirror—
as bright and reassuring,
as quickly gone.

Then back in the tunnel again,
forced back inside the stubborn heart
on the bullet train of the years
hurtling through the darkness
of an old and foreign night, a tunnel
where—however brightly lit the car
in which you sit, bragging of awareness
to others as preoccupied as you—
out there, behind the pane, nothing is
revealed; regression into dark and loss,
and staring blankly back
your own estranged, familiar face
congealed in speeding glass.

Gaijin Lament

Nothing moves inside, only the breeze
shifting through the white lace at the window
and the doors, moving through the rooms
in the same deft way it always did.
But flesh moves here with a difference—
the slick schools of fish, skin silver
and fins black, glide
in unison, slide through the shallows
of the streets, intent, keeping us strange
orange and gold and sickly spotted
carp in the cold of the Emperor's moat.
Is that what makes this heaviness,
this listless craving food does not appease?
Some sorrow is compounded here
where sense slides, like a fish, from the grasp—
just as you feel the cold muscle thrash
in your hand, whatever it was, is gone.

Maybe we broke too many habits all at once
or maybe not enough. But the fingers
that held us clinging
to the last fringes
of meaning, lost their grip . . .
in this new emptiness, we must at last admit

it was not this cause or that, not Church
or bleeding lamb, not Plato and his late lamented
love, nor the subject/object split
nor lure of capital, nor Euclid's rule
nor all we hoped had been the cause
and so, once cured, could clear the air
and heal the soul: but here, our old excuses fail
for here they don't apply, and yet
here too, the same as there

an unrepentant angry core burns hot
as if the planet bore an image in each soul:
cool without and deep within, the fire—
the molten glowing core that when held in
burns like a knife turned in the guts
or, flowing out, lays waste the world
leaves just a trail of char
for rain to settle into mud, for grass
to hold as best it can, persistent
in its sad small flimsy roots,
its chancy flowers.

High Noon at Los Alamos

To turn a stone
with its white squirming
underneath, to pry the disc
from the sun's eclipse—white heat
coiling in the blinded eye: to these malign
necessities we come
from the dim time of dinosaurs
who crawled like breathing lava
from the earth's cracked crust, and swung
their tiny heads above the lumbering tons
of flesh, brains no bigger than a fist
clenched to resist the white flash
in the sky the day the sun-flares
pared them down to relics for museums,
turned glaciers back, seared Sinai's
meadows black—the ferns withered, the swamps
were melted down to molten mud, the cells
uncoupled, recombined, and madly
multiplied, huge trees toppled to the ground,
the slow life there abandoned hope,
a caterpillar stiffened in the grass.
Two apes, caught in the act of coupling,
made a mutant child
who woke to sunlight wondering, his mother
torn by the huge new head
that forced the narrow birth canal.

As if compelled to repetition
and to unearth again
white fire at the heart of matter—fire
we sought and fire we spoke,
our thoughts, however elegant, were fire
from first to last—like sentries set to watch
at Argos for the signal fire
passed peak to peak from Troy
to Nagasaki, triumphant echo of the burning

city walls and prologue to the murders
yet to come—we scan the sky
for that bright flash,
our eyes stared white from watching
for the signal fire that ends
the epic—a cursèd line
with its caesura, a pause
to signal peace, or a rehearsal
for the silence.

Nandin's Tail

—for Sujata Bhatt

As the sun comes up on the suffering world
the stone gods writhe along the twisted
columns on the temple wall, a cliff
the weather sculpted with its hundred tongues.
Within, a blunt stone phallus prods
the blue dusk of the inner shrine, while
at its door, adoring, Nandin, the sweet
devoted cow-eyed Brahma bull, kneels
worshipping the power throbbing
in the Shiva-stone.
And everywhere, the eyes—black
as watermelon seeds, as countless.

While double-natured Shiva dances
along the colonnades of whirling cosmic dust
comets streaming from his outspread hair,
the galaxies a storm of gnats,
deep in the cow-mind of Nandin, a different
figure wanders, losing herself
among the thick and dripping leaves
enormous as the ears of elephants, until
it isn't clear
which is forest shadow and which
her darkening shape. Shiva exhales a last
exhausted breath, lies down among
the ruined worlds he has unmade, strands
of his torn hair like rivers tangled
in his hands, the planets smashed like berries
on the moss below his still white form.

With a racket of bones, her necklace
of skulls swinging over her hanging breasts
Kali leaps and pounds the inert god
her feet pestles of brass, her laughter

rattling in her throat like dry seeds
in a gourd. And Shiva stirs, his pallor
brightens, his belly fills with air.
He rises as the double-god again, he
whose other half is woman; blue-breasted maiden
on the right; left side, a youth whose beard
is just beginning. It all comes round again—
the slow dance of the planets, the great wheel
humming in the sky, the rivers
spreading toward the sea
as the uncoiling cobra spreads its hood and hisses
rising toward the red-soaked altar
of the dawn.

I shake my head and wish it all
away—the tail of Nandin swishing
to brush off flies—and listen
to the whisper of the maple leaves
stirring at the glass, the rush
of passing cars, the comforting hiss
of tires on concrete—and listening so
to what is close, I miss
the clang of worlds colliding
resounding brass beyond our little reach
cymbals
in what we only dream
are hands.

The Towers of Silence

1   Lost with the sun in a chartreuse wood, afflicted
by associations, flies, thirst, and by
a growing chill my clothes cannot keep
out, the path narrowing as I go
like a road in a Roethke poem, taking you out
that long peninsula, the one with the snow, the sand, the ruts
in which your wheels stick
while the headlights darken, flicker and go out . . .

though without a vehicle
and going on foot, I know those roads
today, on the brightest day of early
winter, when the sun makes much of the few
gold leaves still clinging to the branch
as if setting an example
that one could attain, with the slightest
effort, a great cheerfulness—
nevertheless, it is then
that the road starts to narrow
and the sides, closing in, are lined
with something dark like stands of evergreen
but with the hard reflective sheen of polished
stone, like the shining black marble walls
of the Vietnam monument, where, hard as you
strain to understand, you see nothing
but your own face reflected back
scarred with the names
of the dead.

2   And now the towers of silence rise
as if the dead-end path had suddenly
turned and opened on a vast landscape
of sand where silent towers wait, circled
by birds, endlessly circled.

Far out on such a wide, bleached plain
the merciful Zoroastrians raise
their towers, so high the silence
dominates the plain. Up there
they place their dead, the bodies
exposed on platforms
against a vacancy of blue,
and leave them for the birds.

Uncanny, those towers standing so aloof
so silent with their ruined cargo
from a voyage that is past, and the birds
too high and far away for us to hear
their cries; there is only the slow
inexorable orbit of appetite,
centripetal, as if each bird were tied
by invisible string
to the protractor of some immense
geometer, the sharply drawn circle of
the buzzard, condor, kite.

3 "Stay with the body,"
    the last mortality out here
    where the West begins, high
    in the mountain pass, where the cold will keep
    the body till the rescue comes. "Stay
    with the body." Though the chill deepens
    and duty, that binds us here, makes us
    harder and harder to tell
    from what we guard, slowly being covered
    by the kindness of snow, like Antigone's
    deliberate scattering of the dust of Thebes
    to preserve the form of a beloved
    brother. Yet, as the play unfolds
    and even as she argues with the king,
    the dogs and birds, like messengers
    from an older god, disturb the dust, begin

the slow dispersal of Polyneices
through the polis, fragments
taken to the altars and the hearths
and while she bids her bridal hopes farewell
the human body, centered in the circle
like Leonardo's famous figure on the rack
of art, is slowly torn apart. And while
she leaves the light behind forever, you can hear
the cries of birds almost like triumph
the snarling of the dogs in argument
over what each one will have.

4   Out toward the periphery
at the border of what is bearable
where detachment rules,
the Towers of Silence stand.
Now, on those platforms the past is being
picked clean, purified by air and
distance, for it all happens at such a height,
so far away—it could be Plato's dream:
a perfect circle in the sky—except
it moves, it turns, and so shifts to another
text, becomes the wheel of Heraclitus
the transformation of a cast-off flesh
into the winged messengers
of change. And I wonder

if after the magical three days
when the platforms are empty, the birds
risen from the dead and flown, the circle
broken, nothing left but the brilliant
white bones, the sky stripped
of everything but blue—

if with a sigh or a shudder
of release, the watchers turn away, anxious
to move on, climb on their kneeling camels
feel the strange, humped flesh
back under them as it gathers itself up and,
like a minor earthquake, its hills
lurch, shudder and lift, the horizon
suddenly shifting—then they're off
in that wild pitch and roll
of the camel's gait on sand,
growing smaller and smaller, unless

here, we decide to leave the poem
and go with them
because they carry their own water
because the land is dry, the sun hot
and our need for company acute
when, from our own silent towers,
we come down alive.

IV Returns

Classical Proportions of the Heart

Everyone here knows how it ends, in the stone
amphitheatre of the world, everyone
knows the story—how Jocasta
in her chamber hung herself for shame
how Oedipus tore out his eyes and stalked
his darkened halls crying
aaiiee   aaiiee   woe   woe is me   woe

These things everyone expects, shifting
on the cold stone seats, the discomfort
of our small, hard place in things
relieved by this public show of agony
how we love this last bit best, the wait
always worth it: the mask with its empty eyes
the sweet sticky horror of it all
the luxurious wailing, the release
the polis almost licking its lips,
craning our necks to make out the wreck—
the tyrant brought low, howling,
needing at last to lean
on a mere daughter, Antigone, who
in the sequel will inherit
her father's flair for the dramatic
her mother's acquaintance with death;
her hatred of falsehood, her own.

We feel a little superior, our seats
raised above the circle where the blinded
lion paces out his grief, self-condemned,
who could not keep his mastery to the end
(so Creon taunts him). What a flush
of pleasure stains our faces then
at the slow humiliation of an uncommon man
a Classical Golgotha without God, only
an eyeless wisdom, Apollo useless
against age, guilt, bad temper

and, most of all, against Laius
whose fear twisted the oracle's tongue,
child-hater, the father who started it all.

The same night, as the howls rose
from the palace of Oedipus, the crowd
rising, drawing on their cloaks to go home,
far from the stage, that dramatic circle
that fixed our gaze, out there
on the stony hills gone silver under the moon
in the dry Greek air, the shepherd sits
he who saved the baby from the death
plotted by Laius, he who disobeyed a king
for pity's sake. Sitting there alone
under the appalling light of the stars
what does he think of how the gods
have used him, used his kind heart
to bait the trap of tragedy?
What brief can he make for mercy
in a world that Laius rules?

Sitting there, the moon his only audience,
perhaps he weeps, perhaps he feels
the planetary chill alone out there
on what had been familiar hills.
Perhaps he senses still the presence
of the Sphinx. And maybe
that is when he feels the damp
nudge against his hand.
By reflex, we could guess, he reaches out
to touch the coat of wool, begins
to stroke the lamb. "It's late," he says
at last, and lifts the small beast
to his chest, carrying it down
the treacherous stony path toward home, holding
its warmth against him. There is little drama

in this scene, but still its pathos has
a symmetry, because the lamb's small heat
up close exactly balances
the distant icy stars
and when it senses home, and bleats,
its small cry weighs against
the wail of fallen kings.
There is, as well, the perfect closure
as the shepherd's gate swings shut
and a classical composure
in the way he bears
the burden of his heavy heart
with ease.

A Tale That's Best for Winter

This morning they raised the stones.
Methir and I, being children, only
watched, while the stones grew
like mushrooms from the earth after rain.
The big elms stood and watched along with us
and wrist-thick vines, twisted into Celtic knots,
wrestled with each other for the branches at the top
where the view is longest out to sea
across whose waves the largest stones come in
on boats from where the eye goes gray
and mother says that there are other earths like ours
beyond the waters. But those I've never
seen, nor Methir either. Though you'd
hardly know what he had seen, for brothers
don't talk much, and Methir never. They say
girls talk because the gods put honey
on their tongues when they're still budding
in their mothers, but those are only stories.

I, who've seen men sweat to raise the stones
to build the houses for the gods, suspect
the gods of being weak, too little, or too much
like air to raise the stones themselves.
But when I tell my mother this
she looks around, eyes scared, and hits me
where it hurts and says I mustn't
or the rain will turn to fire and burn us
shapeless where we stand. And I have seen
the fire from the sky come down
and split a living tree and leave it like
a dead snake's tongue, a stiff black thing
to stand against the sky. Was it because
the leaves were always whispering, like me,
the things they oughtn't say? When I asked
Methir what he thought, as usual,
he said nothing, either way.

My brother isn't quite like other boys, the ones
who shout and race about, throw stones,
who fight until the red runs out
and I feel sick—my thoughts are dark and dreadful
and it is hard to make them fit together
or else they fit too tight
so I can't see what might be there behind them—
and now I'll tell you what I am afraid of.

The silence of the stones.
The way they stand unmoving in their circles,
giants who are blind to one another, and when
the men are building shelters for the gods
and shelves to put the dead on, I think I see
the stones begin to lean, and then to totter
the men being crushed like beetles—
everything goes black, a shadow like a poet's
curse, a blight in the foretelling
then dry as ink beneath the blotter
as if the rock were on me, its weight
all there was of heaven—up above
the sky is dark and starless.

I like the stars, you see, because they're so
at home in darkness, like foxes
in the bushes, their eyes look out
but all the rest is safely hidden, and the moon
who is their mother, watches out
though sometimes, when she's angry, turns away
until she's scarcely more than edges.
But when she's full-face looking down, the fields
turn silver, the sea fills up with milk
and seems to soften. And though they say the stones
are put out in their circles
to track her path across the heavens
she's much too far away for them to catch her.
So I don't worry. Besides, the stones are eyeless
and brute-stupid as a boar that's cornered.
I saw one once, all growls and mutter, red-eyed

mad, who threw himself straight at my father's
spear as if he'd be the one to do the throwing
though it was himself he threw away
on the long stone blade my father held there waiting.

*   *   *

Today they finished the house of stones
with its great lintel and the bones inside
and then began the digging of the trenches
whose dirt they used to cover up the building
until the barrow stretched for miles, hiding
what was under, like something happened
that you can't remember, but you know it's there
because you have to walk around it. Tonight
the priest put on the deer skull
with the antlers, the women went inside
the sky was dark, the moon in hiding
you could hear the sea but couldn't see it
a cold wind came up and made the trees
go slightly crazy, the hounds all
turned their muzzles up and howled. Men say
the dead are safe now in their houses
under earth, but I think they are angry
and wish they could look out at us
like stars. Sometimes I think the earth inside
is burning, burning with those eyes
that want to see, and are prevented.

The men have gathered by the circle of the stones.
The clouds like old smoke melt and vanish
the moon is round and bright and close
to perfect. And now—oh gods—a great round shield
of black is sliding over . . . the moon is going out.

I cry out, and the men can't help
but hear me; they drag me out
and Methir with me . . . I call up to the moon
to help us, but she is gone
behind that awful shield of black.

82

The men are all in robes and hooded,
they look exactly like the standing stones.
The tallest one is lifting his stone axe above me.
I see it first in Methir's eyes, and then
far off, the edge of ocean flashes, moves in silver—
the moon is coming back. She must have felled the one
who held the shield of black, who couldn't stand
her shining. The men, forgetting us, look up . . .
while they stand lost in heaven's spiral
I take Methir's hand, we run together
down the cliff path to the coast
we take the little boat tied to a tree there
and raise the sail into the winter wind.
"Methir, there are other earths
beyond the waters, mother says so, we will go
there." And Methir, who never spoke before, says
"Yes. I know the way." And takes the tiller.

             *   *   *

How many years have gone since then? How many
ports slid past our bow? How many moons
were swallowed by earth's shadow?
How many miles to find it
everywhere the same: the riven tree,
the hooded stones, the bloody sanction
given. Better to go back
where we know the woods, where the words are fitted
to our tongues, where we know the hiding places
and the names. Better to take the tiller back
and turn the boat for home.

I watch the cliffs loom up along our coast
as Methir stares into the silence
out of which he came.
And the sighing in the shrouds
is like the harp—old "goddess
with gold ribs"—her strings stretched
taut against the night, her song is
heaven crying, or it is us, or wind.

Sunset on the Pembrokeshire Cliff Path

—in loving memory, Norman Harris, a king in a stone cottage

The sky poised on the point
of land, like a stone slab on a megalith,
as if the sea-mirrored sky, all light
rested on a single point
called Wales, your place
where all our history seems a blink
to such a clock as that stone cliff
and old earth is, or that still slower
going of the sun, burning low towards dusk
when twilight pours its cream
into the churn of sea, the dying wind will stir
the colors in—the coral, dusty rose and
gold; the line of hills a phrase
of music with its rise and fall
on land's great single theme of green.

The little boats at anchor rock in the amber
sun, each one a buoy of light; a few still
make for shore, their sails furled,
motors purring like a cat deep in its fur.
High on the velvet turf, over
the quiet sea, we watch the sun grow
lower, melt into the water, dusk obscure
the old division of the sky
from sea, till you can't tell
what glides on water from what rides
the air, a black bird
with a band of gold around its throat
soars in the in-between
and all that is awry comes right
balanced on the last of light
the restless heart
come home
at last
to rest

*

84

On the Place of Theory
in an Obsolete Poetics

What appears to be a stable, tangible, audible world is an illusion (Maya).
What we normally see is the explicate or unfolded order of things. But
there is an underlying order that is father to this second-generation
reality.

> —in a letter from a friend who went west,
> quoting Marilyn Ferguson quoting David Bohm

This blooming, buzzing world may be
(or is) illusion, and we are only
second-generation stuff, the daughters
of some fathering and implicate design
(e.g., see Plato). And when I touch
the velvet of a fawn or the soft wool
of some poor phantom lamb, it is pure
romance that I feel
these whirling atoms on my thumb
as gentleness enfolded in the heart,
that fat red tireless muscle
posing as an image of emotion—
merely the commotion of
the hormones, a chemical solution
for what a starving mystic sometimes
takes for God. Or, being poor and mortal,
when lying flat out in a meadow
(concatenation of chlorophyll and light)
I see the golden flowers—extravagantly
yellow—as many-petalled joy
unfolded in the grass, though joy
is merely floods of epinephrin
and flowers have no color but rather
the sort of molecules to gather
certain wavelengths of the light
as bees will gather nectar
never stopping to consider
how like Mendel in his garden

they behave, pollen clinging
to the hair on their small legs,
unstable matter merely following
a coded message. So their cells fill up
with honey, as sweet as any error
made by our clumsy senses,
as a poet will mistake
the marks on paper saying *honey*
for an amber liquid
that delights the tongue. Oh, we are fooled
as any crowing rooster who imagines
his song brings up the sun.
Enough to make you smile—a flash
of calcium in the parted tissue
of our lies. So we, thigh-deep
in our illusions, like a booted fisherman
up to his crotch in mud and water,
will hurl our slender lines where fish
are leaping, as if our lines were really
there, as if we could reel in
a solid, silver-scaled something
who looks straight at us
with a rather desperate eye,
as if the implicate, enfolded order
of the universe (that cosmic larva)
were not more real than this minute—
these fins still flapping in a panic
like a pair of wings, as if
this too-thin air could once again
be water, and she be there,
back in it.

Looking Back at Yeats

The sun in the leaves again. Yeats stares
at me, incorrigibly young, through his gold-rimmed
glasses, in black and white, an oval portrait
on the cover of the Collier paperback, an egg
from which the past is hatching; tomorrow,
like red marrow, forced back into the bone.
While the wind howls wild on the western coast
of Ireland, the horses, unprotected, graze
the long sliver of green that juts
like a moss-grown tongue from the rocky shore,
exiled by the ruined walls
of ancient farm and fortress, the scent
of horseflesh on the fog-soaked wind,
the cloying smell of burning peat
that clogs the lungs, the manor house
a shell, the past curled up inside—dying
to be born. And Yeats regards
the present from his fixed position
on the book, his mouth a little open,
his white collar prim as a parson's,
today reproved forever in his slightly
timid gaze. Today, the sun here in the maple,
the clear return of autumn, the browning
of the green, the turn of leaves
to burnished yellow, ornaments
from the age of gold, an age
that's now or never.

It was no better then, I swear, staring
back at Yeats. Only the mind,
led by the heart's barbed lure,
casting backwards, grows
ingenuous where it never had to live,
catches the glint
of sun on rusted armor, thinks it gold,

dreams the poet called the tune, breathes
a softening haze on the distant mirror,
as the lute and the ballad try it again,
fountains in the pouring rain
playing the same old redundant refrain
to the same unoriginal sin.

It's Not Cold Here

—for Bob

Somewhere the flags are frozen
in the bitter wind and cannot flap,
the brittle trees stand outlined in the ice,
black relics in glass cases, back-lit
by the sickly light of a fitful sun;
somewhere the drifts of snow are studded
with those who didn't make it home,
who died embedded in the white
where they sought cover; somewhere, water
falling slow over the stone rift
in the mountain, froze solid
and hangs in air like some perfected dogma . . .

but it's not cold here
although outside it's winter—
this place we never chose, but only
found, as luck would have it,
as mountain streams, impetuous and cold,
flow down but with no way of knowing
how slow they'd grow and brown
on broad alluvial plains.
Too much is made of choice:
we merely came the way we could
being what we were, and we were changed
by the terrain we came by. Nor could we
see around a single bend
until we'd turned it. And it was wind
and not a course we'd charted
that brought us to a pebbled shore
whose stones the sea had shaped and
polished, and gave us food we'd never
tasted. Of this, we had no premonition
nor even, quite, desire;

though we may dream of fire
when lost in ice, the temperate zones
are never those we dream of, the mind
proceeding by extremes, desire by contrast.

And now it's hard to say just where we are
except it isn't cold here
the light is often amber
we can't remember
the sting of wind-whipped snow
against the eyes nor the stop-frame
of the ice. Here we are happy,
forgetful of the cold—as well-fed children,
dragging sleds, see every snowbound hill
as heaven, made just to climb
for the pure abandoned joy of sliding down.

"Midway the journey of this life . . ."
—for Vicky

we reach a place without a border
on the past, for no one
walks here hot with hate
trying to unwind her soul
from the sharp spindle of childhood
when she was held
by other hands, and spun and twisted
on the narrow stick. Here
there is a slow turning in a bright air,
but it is not that counter-spin
with which we all begin. Not now. Not anymore.
Nor is this nostalgia's realm
whose citizens keep stumbling into what is lost,
regrets half-buried in the grass,
so every forward step is a little turning back.

No. Here the place itself is ancient
beyond our count, deep in that other history
of trees, their roots sunk under walls
until they pull them down, leaving
a scatter of stones, as if some epic
game were interrupted, the pieces dropped
in the grass, and the point mislaid.
For everyone but the simple
and the wise, who never saw the point, forgot
what the wall was for,
though many brought their stones to it
and the small mortar of their hopes.

Now, where so much is undisclosed,
there is suggestion in the air, a stir
so light it moves us, for we are
airy now as a veil of lace,

sheer enough for the light
to pass straight through, as if we were
no thicker than our skins.

And the scattered stones, strewn here
and there, no longer can be called
ruins—the dying fall of such a word demands
desire for a past that stands
still between us and the sun.
The stones instead seem the runes
of grass, some arcane statement
that the field is making.

As a seed that's winged
with soft white down is borne aloft,
it neither seeks the ground nor thinks
of growing, it is the most abandoned, freest
thing, it floats the way
wind veers and may land anywhere,
take root, or simply rot.
Mere bits of breathing, downy stuff,
so many, such a multitude—the earth
will catch enough of us to make a spring,
while those blown down on water or on sand
will decorate the surface like a snow,
dress all the world in momentary lace,
so whether we end
in use, we end in beauty, moved as if
in trance, the flight has stirred us and
the open air become a scroll
for the slow, unwinding spiral of our dance.

Still Waters

When the sun strikes
the roe, translucent pearls
of orange, and turns them
to a mass of fire, the little fish—
like the first silver flicker
of some world-changing notion—spin off
into the cold, uprushing current
where it leaves the bordered pool
and pours into the river. Swift
particles of light that swirl together
like a ray, flit here and there as if
to shed a slender light on what is
hidden. The change we know: a loss
of easiness, the way pure water
seems to grow too thin, some
alteration in the gills or in the genes,
a splitting off of single
purpose from the little school
that moved as one. And then surrender
to the river, that absent-minded rush
downstream, through rapids, boiling
in the grip of boulders, the long fall
when all feeling leaves you,
the tossed arrivals in the churning
foam below where fins seem
mere redundancy of nature, the power
all outside you, growing
as you go. Everything says ocean,
ocean—obsessive thought that's all
propulsion and no form. Something begins
to happen to the water, as if shed tears
had fed it, a new solution
with a way of clouding light.
You pass into the semi-darkness, dim shapes
of monsters gliding by you: everywhere
you look—the open jaws.

Years pass, and how to count them?
years of slowly picking out
the shapes while sliding by them, naming
in the moment of evasion:
shark, stingray, moray eel.
Knowing danger by its shadows—
the gulls that hover in the shallows,
the terns that fall like arrows,
everything is feint and parry, this ocean
that you burned to enter
will only let you live
by indirection as perpetual
as motion, while what you feed on
sometimes comes to look
like what you were.

You learn, at last, to hate
the crooning voice of ocean, the stupid
sirens with their deadly
lullabies, the rise and fall
of waves like nations, the booming
on the rocks—monotonous artillery
of tides. A fugitive from
ocean's murk and its titanic
nightmares, an old desire for quiet
reawakens—as the mind begins
to gather for its leap
toward clear pools in the lap
of sheltering mountains, the warm orange
light that once ignited
has begun again to smoulder
like some rekindling ember
of the sun, or glowing autumn,
until, remembering, you swerve away
from the swollen dream that men
imagine ocean, take heart
and, strong against the current,
head upstream.

The Green Connection

—in celebration of Trudy and Michael

When the vein of jade is opened
in the spring, winter's icy hasp
pried loose—the lid comes off the universe
of carp, just where the sun is looking
with its long warm gaze of gold
the frozen vein begins to flow again
as a line of song, learned by heart as a child,
forgotten for years, runs again
in the mind, the melting jade
begins to slide, crowding its shores
spreading out, starting to pour
down the long, falling curve
of the young mountain, filling
as it goes, a long green song of water
recalling itself, as a scroll of fern
unrolls in the first spring sun, turning
the hard rock of the heights
into a lyrical passage, light moving
through shade into waiting—
the rains expected soon
the rice paddies will fill again
the squares of mud become mirrors
sprouting green, as if reflection
on its own could grow, as if the sky
had come to rest down here
and in between, the shoots of green that grow
from what has been to what will be

the grains of rice
whose polish and the steam
make them glisten in the bowl
the delicate white of porcelain, rice paper
shoji screens, each square aglow
with light, shine like pearls in water

back home, night's black impasto
scraped off by the flat palette knife
of dawn, a pair of shutters
suddenly thrown wide, and from
the open window at the center of the man
a woman leans out, calling
to the brightening day
and sees a pair of white cranes float
across the miles of sky, across
the frame of the painter's eye, to where
the snow is still thick on the peaks
of Asagai, while in our garden here
in Hatsudai, the rough and twisted trunk
succumbs to spring, and overnight
unfolds its bridal silks
of plum.

—Tokyo, 1986

Conversation with a Japanese Student

That lovely climbing vine, so fresh
at dawn, so shy at noon, whose blue
countenance we call Morning Glory, you
call it *asakao,* Morning Face.
"What is this glory?" you ask, child
of *akarui,* even the memory of war
effaced. "What is it all *for?*"

            *   *   *

Here is an artist working, his brush
is history's tongue, his canvas
allegorical and large, the landscape
must be ample for his theme—
the turn of epic tides, pulled
in the wake of a dream. Glory,
unlike her homely twin, Mortality,
casts no shadow, never rests
("A beautiful and charming Female
floating Westward through the air,
bearing on her forehead
the Star of Empire"). There,

notice that Glory is artfully draped
in a tunic of pale silk in the Classical style
her limbs as plump and supple
as oil paint and appetite
can make them, the lift of her head—proud,
a summons and a dare, one delicious arm
carries a bright banner streaming in the air
its design illegibly wrought
with large suggestions. But of Glory
you can be sure because
an army marches in her train—
almost a shadow, darkening the land.
At times, a peasant woman
raising her gaunt baby in a trite appeal
may momentarily block the light, obscure
Glory, put a little in the shade

all that golden beauty
the toss of whose curls is worth
a thousand ships, a million
villages, the world

for even a glimpse, the faintest rustle
of the hem of Beatrice's skirt
as it disappears around the corner
of those gates of pearl to the eternal
harbor, the flutter of doves
in the white thighs of Helen, desire
in its perfected form. The mirror of art
becomes a burning glass in the light
of absolute desire, the brush a flame
about to be consumed, for he has reached
the limits, here, of art—as Michelangelo
one night when he was old, in his rage
at the stubborn stone's refusal
to yield to his conception, attacked
his last Pietà with his chisel
trying to tear the pattern from the matter,
Christ from the arms of his grieving
mother; his servant
was forced to subdue the master
in order to save the work.

This time, no servant soul to intervene
and fire at the core, the center
split—as if mankind, with its cold
forever mind, trapped in its furious, failing heart
had torn the Pietà apart from within—gone
the mother, a cloud of glowing dust,
gone the son, dissolved
in the monstrous cloud, heaven's fungus
growing on the axis of the world
casting its white shadow on the hills
pitiless as any parasite
whose life depends
on what it slowly kills.

No brush can paint a light so pure
         only the blind can see   white hot
     it whites out everything   but what is not
          the sun's high noon, but brighter . . .
"ex Occidente, lex; ex Oriente, lux"
        out of the West, law; out of the East, light.
        *   *   *
At Nagasaki in the Peace Park near
the epicenter of the blast
there is a glade
so dense with foliage, bushes, *asakao*
and pine, you'd almost miss the sign, hand-drawn,
the only one in English that I saw:

THEY SAID NOTHING WOULD GROW HERE
    FOR 75 YEARS

And though the language was my own
I found it difficult to read
through such a thick exquisite screen
of evergreen
and tears.

Having Eaten of the Tree of Knowledge

On the plains of Thessaly
where the wheat had begun again
its season, a fresh wind tore
the wreath of clouds from Mt. Olympus,
the sun picked out the peak of naked rock
and kindled it. The horses grazing
placid in green pastures, looked up
with liquid eyes as fathomless as dreams
and though we'll never know
it was as if they might have thought
of Chiron, wise centaur, wounded
by his half that was the human,
who traded his Olympian situation,
the immortality of gods and
monsters, for death
to heal an old division.

So we come down from stony haunts—
the hypothetical eternal—to find another
way into the garden, not by the gate
guarded by the iron angel. Nor shall we
call it by the ancient name. After so long
an exile, what have we to do with Edens?
Bred on the bitter fruit of choice, having
soaked the earth with the dragon's blood
pouring from our mortal wounds—
this time we'll pick the other Tree
and eat the fruit of life.

Notes

"Time Out of Mind" owes not only its epigraph but the idea that "we come after the dream" to George Steiner's *Language and Silence*.

"Never apologize for poetry" was something Vernon Young said to me after a poetry reading. His discussion of Robinson Jeffers's line, "I hate my verses," originally provoked this poem.

"Into the distance where all things reverse and touch" is taken from Mary Kinzie's "Where the Storm Goes," from *The Threshold of the Year* (University of Missouri Press, 1982), p. 45.

In "Beauty and the Beast" the quoted line, "These things in which we have seen ourselves and spoken" is from Richard Wilbur's poem "Advice to a Prophet."

The word "*gaijin*" in "*Gaijin* Lament" means "foreigner" or "outsider" in Japanese. The word, as elsewhere, and probably everywhere, is pejorative.

The reference in "High Noon at Los Alamos," "sentries set to watch/ at Argos for the signal fire," is to the opening scene of *Agamemnon* by Aeschylus.

The source of the line in part 3 of "The Towers of Silence," "Stay with the body" (and the sense of it as the rock bottom frontier ethic) is Joan Didion's essay, "On Morality," this passage in particular: "One of the promises we make to one another is that we will try to retrieve our casualties, try not to abandon our dead to the coyotes. If we have been taught to keep our promises . . . we stay with the body, or have bad dreams." In *Slouching toward Bethlehem* (Farrar, Straus & Giroux, 1968), p. 158.

In "Looking Back at Yeats," the image of "the distant mirror" both borrows the title and refers to the substance of Barbara Tuchman's book demystifying medieval knighthood; in Richard Hugo's words, "Something right goes wrong/with brutality when it loses history and style."

The phrase "shine like pearls in water" in "The Green Connection" is from Sam Hamill's translation of Lu Chi's *Wen Fu* (*The Art of Writing*), published by Breitenbush Press, 1987.

In "Conversation with a Japanese Student," *akarui* is a compound word meaning "clear" and "bright." Generally used to refer to a fine day, its extended meaning denotes the bright time of peace and prosperity in Japan since the 1960s.

The quotation in that poem ("A beautiful and charming Female floating Westward through the air, bearing on her forehead the Star of Empire") appeared in the text on the reverse side of "American Progress," a popular allegorical print of 1873. The print shows Indians, horses, buffalo and bear ("on the left we find darkness, waste and confusion") fleeing before the various avatars of "Progress": frontier guide, hunter, farmer . . pony express, wagon, railroad . . . cities, schools, churches ("The grand drama of Progress in the civilization, settlement and history of our own happy land"). The presiding white, diaphanous figure in the center is the "Female floating Westward" of the original quotation. (Image and text appear in *The Incorporation of America: Culture and Society in the Gilded Age* by Alan Trachtenberg.) The version of that figure which most vividly haunts the poem, however, is probably Delacroix's "Liberty Leading the People," 1848. In 1849 Delacroix said to George Sand: "This liberty won at so high a price is not true liberty."